Ou

A tale of two egg-donor children

by Gina Hashrard

First published in August 2014.

ISBN-13: 978-1500763619

ISBN-10: 1500763616

Author's note: I have tried to recreate events, locations and conversations from my memories of them. In order to maintain their anonymity in some instances I have changed the names of individuals and places, and I may have changed some identifying characteristics and details. Gina Hashrard is a pseudonym.

For Beaver and Norman,

never forgetting Scruffy and Slow.

INTRODUCTION

"I'd do anything to have children", my husband said firmly, on our way to Christine's wedding.

We'd been discussing it for a while by now. I wasn't exactly *old*. We'd married when I was 34, which I admit is no spring chicken, but still... 2 years later I was under the knife losing my right ovary, and 4 months after that I suffered a post-surgical menopause. We had been told this meant we couldn't have the children we'd been hoping and trying for since our wedding night.

I'd been devastated when we had the news. Probably most annoying was Seamus's persistent optimism that everything would be fine. He didn't seem to *get* it. It was bad enough coping with my own grief, without having to manage the apparent idiocy of an imbecilic husband who hadn't grasped the facts of non-life yet. To his eternal credit, he underwent the screaming, sobbing, pummelling and door-slamming with grim determination. I genuinely believed that divorce was the best way forward. Why thwart his dreams of fatherhood just because I couldn't deliver the goods? I just wanted to cut him free and let him have the children I knew he needed to have. I don't mean to suggest I was unhinged – although looking back now, perhaps I was, just a little!

Our appointment at the Oxford Fertility Unit (OFU) rolled around, and I went with more than a touch of pessimism in my heart. I think I was bracing myself for the fall-out when Seamus was finally told by a professional that all hope was lost, and he realised that his persistent optimism was useless. Only it didn't quite work out like that. I can't remember the exact conversation that led to the revelation that we might be able to have children after all, but I do remember that I left the building feeling bewildered and happy – and with a very jubilant husband. We had options now, and we just needed to decide what we wanted to do. We could have children, and I could bear them, but they wouldn't have my genetic input.

So here we were. My husband would do anything to have children. Clearly the expectation was that I would do anything too. Was I willing to do this?

1.

I had always assumed I would have children. I never went through a stage of life thinking that my career would be too important to interrupt with motherhood, and I never screwed up my nose at the idea of having a baby. As I hit 30 and became more successful in my work (if not in my love-life – I was 32 when I first laid eyes on the man who was to become my husband) people would sometimes comment on the fact that I was an unmarried career woman, and I would blithely reply that I just wasn't ready yet. I was conventional enough to believe that marriage should precede parenthood, and I was very focussed on my work. Nevertheless, I had always assumed I would have children. At some point.

When I met my husband Seamus, he was the sweetest and kindest man I had ever known. Seamus was very open about the fact that he wanted children, and I was happy to admit the same. I was fairly sure that whoever was fortunate enough to have him as a father would be the luckiest child in the world. He was energetic and fun and, as I said already, sweet and kind. If anyone had been born into the world to be a father figure, it was him.

Seamus asked me to marry him within a couple of months of meeting, and I unhesitatingly said yes.

We were married just after I turned 34. Having been together for nearly 2 years by this stage we both felt we would be happy to have children straight away. Therefore, from our wedding night onwards, we stopped all forms of contraception and kept our fingers crossed.

Nothing happened. (Well, okay, quite a lot happened, and of course it was marvellous, but the anticipated result of conception did not!)

After a year or so I went to my doctor. I admit that I exaggerated the amount of time we had been trying to conceive in order to get some attention sooner rather than later (in the UK, the doctors won't investigate unless you say you have been 'trying' for 2 years). My menstrual cycle had never been totally 'normal' in terms of regularity or flow, and I just had a feeling that something wasn't right. However, after months of blood tests on me, and Seamus undergoing a semen test, we were informed that there was nothing obviously wrong and we should keep trying.

The thing about this process is that it does rather take the fun out of the 'trying'. The act of sex is no longer a fun or sensual activity, but a means to an end that was always ultimately disappointing at the end of every month. If I had my time again, I would probably try to ensure that we didn't lose so much of the magic, and that we hadn't let the boredom take us over. I know that these things drop off in all relationships, but I suspect that having gone through this intensely 'functional' stage of your sexual life-cycle puts an additional pressure on the couple concerned. Speaking personally, our own sex life took a very, very long time to recover. Although I'm sure it would have been a price we were both prepared to pay at the time, I can't help thinking that if I had managed the situation a bit better perhaps we might have been able to negotiate a discount!

It also didn't help that I was starting to show a fair bit of spread around my middle, and I was feeling very frumpy and un-sexy anyway. It was my older sister who possibly saved my life. "Look" I said, tapping my growing abdomen and scowling. "I can't seem to shift it. It's rock hard." I had been on a strict 1200-calorie per day diet for about 3 months, yet I was still putting on weight. I had a desk job and was hardly active, but this was starting to feel ridiculous.

She reached out and frowned. "I don't think that's right," she said. "Have you seen anyone about it?" She gave me the number of her gynaecologist. How she had the intuition to do this I will never know, but as I said, it possibly saved my life.

I was in the fortunate position of being in a good situation financially at that time, so thinking I was about to throw a few hundred pounds at a strange man to put my mind (and my sister's) at rest really wasn't a problem back then. This was in the days before you needed a general practitioner's recommendation letter to go and see a specialist in the UK. I was able to just phone up and make an appointment. If I tried to do the same today, I wouldn't be able to do it – I would be required to get a recommendation letter from my general practitioner first, and somehow I doubt that would have been as easy as it sounds, as they had already declared that there was nothing wrong with me! (For your amusement, I could also tell you that as a last try with my general practitioner I booked an appointment to see someone at their surgery in the morning before I went to the private gynaecologist. I pointed out my rock-hard, swollen abdomen and was advised I might be wheat-intolerant...)

Anyway, I arrived at the gynaecologist and within minutes I was being referred for an ultrasound scan. He said he could see exactly what the problem was the moment I walked in the door, but he needed to see how big it was. In fact, it was so big it didn't fit on the ultrasound screen so they couldn't get a measurement. He had me under his knife for an emergency procedure less than 5 days later to cut out the biggest ovarian cystadenoma (a broad term given to a certain types of ovarian epithelial tumours) he had seen. It was over a foot in length, and I was very lucky that it was benign. I was also lucky that it had not burst, and that it had not done any permanent damage to my kidneys or other internal organs.

However, one of my ovaries had to be removed in the operation. I had known this was a risk, so perhaps it wasn't surprising that my first words on waking in the recovery room were, "Can I still have children?" The gynaecologist smiled and assured me that it wouldn't be a problem. He was confident that one ovary would continue to work on its own.

Sadly, he was wrong. Within 4 months I was hot-flushing and blood tests revealed that I had undergone a post-surgical menopause at the age of 36. The gynaecologist no longer smiled as he told me, "No, you cannot have children."

2.

Even in a 'fortunate' financial position, funds do not last forever, so at this point my liaison with private healthcare ended and I returned to my general practitioner. (Not the one who mistook an ovarian tumour for wheat-intolerance; we had a new doctor by this time!) I needed to undergo new blood tests to prove my condition to the National Health Service (NHS; the results of privately-funded existing blood tests were apparently inadequate). This all took more time, as we needed to wait for a particular time in my menstrual cycle to perform the tests, and since my cycles had all but dried up these were few and far between. Finally, about 6 months later, I was put on HRT.

It is difficult to think back now to how I felt at the time. The world is full of women who have been denied their chance of motherhood for one reason or another, and my misery easily equalled the thousands of those who had gone before me. Let's not dwell on that part of the story.

I like to think that I did not begrudge other people their happy families. Certainly I had one or two friends who had children (although most people in my social circle tended to be career women who had not – either by choice or otherwise – had children themselves). I enjoyed spending time with those friends when I could, and I honestly found it interesting to talk to them about their children. I wasn't jealous in a bitter sort of way. I just wished that I could have had the opportunity to live that sort of life too.

Seamus and I discussed the possibility of adoption. His own paternal grandfather had been adopted, and one of his cousins had been adopted from Sri Lanka at the age of 3, so it wasn't an alien concept in his family. However, I wasn't sure how I felt about it. This may be an impolitic and/or selfish viewpoint, but whereas up to the 1960s it was 'nice' girls who had to give up their babies when they had fallen from social grace, my feeling was that nowadays the only children or babies put up for adoption were those with very difficult backgrounds. I wasn't sure how I felt about having a baby who had been borne by a drug addict, for example. It didn't seem to bode well. I realise that some people might think that's a selfish view, and I accept the viewpoint that those babies are the ones who need the most stable upbringing – perhaps they are the ones you could most help to give a normal life. But I wasn't sure I would be able to do it myself.

Around the time I was put on HRT my general practitioner asked if I would like to be referred to a consultant at the local NHS hospital to discuss options for IVF treatment. My understanding from my private gynaecologist was that IVF was no longer an option as I wasn't ovulating. However, my general practitioner – God bless her – persuaded me to go and see someone anyway.

Another few months later (things move slowly!) I turned up for my consultant appointment, not feeling terribly optimistic. I explained the situation to her, and she looked over my records. I wish I could remember her name – she was absolutely lovely. I only met her the once, but she changed my life in that short space of time. "I would like to refer you to an IVF unit," she said. "You have a choice of..." and she reeled off a list of units that I was able to go to.

"Which one would you choose?" I asked her.

She hesitated. It wasn't really a fair question. I knew she wasn't supposed to recommend one unit over the other, but faced with a list of places I knew nothing about, I really didn't see how I could make the right decision myself.

"Well," she eventually replied, "The Oxford Fertility Unit is not-for-profit; it puts back all its profit into research."

"Then I'd like to go to Oxford, please," I said. She smiled at me, and I had a feeling that she thought I'd made the right choice!

Another couple of months, and another appointment – this time in Oxford.

Another explanation of our situation, another semen test for Seamus (they were able to confirm that he had a very, very high sperm count – he was very, very proud!) and another look over my records.

They have a special scanner attachment that looks a bit like a dildo, and that's pretty much what it is. They put a condom over the top, lube it up, and in it goes! (I had been blissfully unaware that such devices existed before this time.) The good news is that the dildo scan doesn't require you to have a full bladder, so you are at least spared the discomfort of bursting for the loo while they push down on your abdomen. Rather, this one needs an empty bladder so they can get a clear view across to your ovaries (or ovary, singular, in my case). My scan showed what we already knew – I was not ovulating, and there was no possibility of harvesting my eggs for IVF treatment.

I had not really allowed myself to get my hopes up, so there were no tears at this stage – just a mental "I told you so" to myself.

However, our nurse Cathy dropped a bombshell. Provided all the tests went okay, we could have children – by egg donation.

I can't have been the first to do this, because the box of tissues was right there, ready and waiting. I just burst into tears.

3.

So, as I was saying, "I'd do anything to have children", my husband said firmly, on our way to Christine's wedding. My husband would do anything to have children. Clearly the expectation was that I would do anything too. Was I willing to do this?

Yes, most definitely. No question!

The first choice we had to make was whether we wanted to stay with the OFU, or move our case to Spain. Apparently a lot of people move over to Spain because it is a lot, lot quicker than staying in the UK on the waiting list for suitable eggs. Since egg donation in Spain is completely anonymous, with no way to later track down the donor, there are many egg donors and virtually no waiting lists. (In the UK, while the donor may be anonymous at the time of donation, when the child reaches the age of 18 he or she has the right to find the egg donor.) We were sorely tempted by the increased speed the Spanish system might offer, and Seamus and I are both quite dark so any Mediterranean input into our child's appearance would not have looked odd. However, we were uncomfortable about the anonymity of donorship. What if our child later wanted to find out about his or her genetic origins? We felt that he or she should have a right to do this at a later stage, and to close a door on all possibility of doing it felt wrong to us.

Having made the decision to stay in the UK for treatment, we needed to undergo a counselling session before starting the process. I was absolutely terrified. What if the counsellor decided I wasn't fit to be a mother, and we weren't allowed to do this after all? (I had no doubt that Seamus would pass with flying colours.) In my head, this was going to be like the world's worst interview, and I was either going to pass or fail. I tried to think of all the questions I might be asked. The main one I was fairly sure they would ask was, "Why do you want a baby?" This little question had me flummoxed. "Because I've always wanted one" just didn't seem to be a good enough answer. The question possessed me for days leading up to the counselling, until at last I had an answer. I just wasn't sure they would think it was a very good, stable answer...

You see, although lots of people want little versions of themselves running around, I wasn't too bothered about that. In fact, to be brutally honest, I wasn't really sure I wanted to pass on some of my genes. On my father's side we have a history of multiple sclerosis, schizophrenia and manic depression (he didn't have the best childhood, poor chap!). My mother's side isn't known to have anything so clinically defined, but throughout the generations there do seem to have been continuous problems with fidelity and stability – nurture or nature? Who knows? But my point is that I didn't have a fantastic family history that I was desperate to pass on to the next generation. On the other hand, Seamus was my life, and I did very much want a little version of him running around my feet. I rolled this answer around in my head on the way to Oxford that day, trying to think how to best articulate these feelings and thoughts without sounding too weird, pathetic or mentally deranged.

I'm sure it's good that I came up with an answer, and it probably helped me to 'know myself better', as the self-help gurus say, but actually the counselling session wasn't like an interview at all, and of course the question of why we wanted a baby never surfaced. (A wonderful thing about the OFU – as I discovered much later by a chance comment dropped by Cathy – is their attitude that it is *everyone's right* to have a baby.) The main point that I remember discussing is when we would tell the baby about his or her genetic origins. My initial response was that I would wait until he or she was old enough to understand, probably as a teenager. I hadn't thought about the hormones and paranoia that come with that time of life ("Everyone hates me!" being the most common phrase on many teenagers' lips), and we were very gently but sensibly advised to raise the child with the knowledge from the start. If they grow up with the knowledge of where they come from, the fact will always be there, ready to be processed when they start to understand the facts of life. This crucial piece of advice has stayed with me. Apart from that, I can't remember very much about the counselling session at all – I was too nervous for most of it to be retained, I'm afraid. Despite it being a test you only had to turn up to in order to pass, I do remember that I was hugely relieved when it was over, and we had the green light to continue!

We joined the waiting list for 'suitable' eggs. "Oh," Cathy sighed, as we told her. "If only you were here a couple of weeks ago, we had the perfect match for you!" Cathy was in charge of matching donors to recipients. On the constant lookout for donor women who look a bit like anyone on her waiting list, all things being equal your 'luck' at your turn coming round depended largely on whether she saw similarities between the two of you. Apparently I had just missed out on a lovely lady of Italian descent (I am 25% Italian) who had the same skin tone, eyes and hair colouring as me. The care and attention that Cathy seems to take over this matching process is incredible. Seamus and I posed for our file photos (for Cathy's later reference) and then we waited.

We waited for 9 months.

4.

Around the time that we went on the waiting list, I had another call that was to drastically affect another area of my life. At the time, my business partner Elliot and I owned our own scientific writing agency. We had started it about 8 years previously, with the aim of having a small, data-focussed company, contrasting with the marketing-focussed agencies that form the mainstay of that service industry. Most of our work comprised trawling through high piles of data from clinical trials and producing technical documents for pharmaceutical companies, universities and research institutes. Over the 8 years, we had slowly grown the company to employ a dozen people, and we were turning a fair profit. We hadn't really given a lot of thought about the long-term future so it came a little out of the blue to discover that we might be ripe for a takeover.

Bizarre though it seemed at the time, there are companies out there that make a living by finding big companies that want to buy small companies, and small companies that are willing to be bought by those big ones. Even now, I don't really know what you would call that sort of business... brokering, maybe? Anyway, Elliot and I were invited to attend a seminar run by this 'brokering' company, and they preached sweet music to our ears. It had not been our intention to sell our agency but, having been presented with this possibility, it didn't seem like a bad idea. There are many reasons that people might want to sell a company, and the one that appealed to me most at the time was the prospect of an 'exit strategy'. Our agency took a huge amount of my time and energy to run and manage, and I had been devoted to it since its inception. Elliot and I both did a lot of international travel, probably being out of the country for two weeks of every four in a typical month. However, as my life was starting to change track, I had begun wondering how I would be able to be the sort of mother that I wanted to be, and retain my required level of performance in the company. The two didn't mesh well, in my mind. Perhaps the answer was to make a neat exit from work, let someone else take the reins, and I could 'retire' to become a full-time mother.

   After the seminar, I explained to Elliot how I was starting to feel. I do not remember telling him the full details of our IVF program, but he had always known that at some point Seamus and I had planned to have children. I suppose he just assumed that the time had come for us to get a move on! Elliot said he wouldn't want to run the company without me (in other words, he didn't want to buy me out himself), and I wasn't really very surprised when he said that in fact he wouldn't mind selling the company at this stage – it was a good little company, showing consistent growth and profit, and all being well we should each make a tidy little sum from our shares. He didn't *quite* have dollar signs running round his eyes, but I don't think either of us could deny the attraction of cashing in our chips at this time!

Therefore, when we received the follow-up call a couple of days later, we agreed to meet with the brokering company's representative, and she helped us through the next few stages of the process. They had a number of potential buyers for us, and we had to meet with all of them. Some were outlandish, like the Greek shipping magnate who came over on a day trip just to meet us and could barely speak English. Some were quite rude, like the man who laid back, linked his fingers behind his head and said "Well, I'm here – impress me." Whether we managed to impress him or not is probably a moot point, but I don't think he was ever a real contender anyway!

In the end, we had three offers on the table, and we had to choose which one to go with. Obviously, the brokering company wanted us to take the highest offer, as they work on commission. However, we took the middle-valued deal. This buyer seemed to appreciate the special values that we had used to shape the company, understood how fond we were of our dozen employees, and promised to invest in the company (as and where it was located at the time) to grow it to bigger and better things in its own image. Elliot and I were to stay on for a year after the deal went through, just to ensure a smooth handover of skills and expertise.

What can I say? We were naïve!

By the end of that year, they had moved the company 30 miles away, upset our key clients, slashed profits and decimated my dream team. It turned out all they really wanted was our blue-chip client base. My staff blamed me, I know. They seemed to think I was in a position to do something about all the nasty changes, but apart from argue and fuss, even knowing that once I was gone at the end of the year whatever I said wouldn't make any difference anyway, there wasn't much that was in my power.

However, it was difficult for me to be too upset about all this by the time. You see, all those meetings with the brokering company and prospective buyers, and all the due diligence and legal steps for the sale? That all took about 9 months.

Days within completing the deal, Cathy called.

5.

By now, I was 39 years old and Seamus was 35. Oh? Did I not mention that he's younger than me? Well, yes, I pulled a younger man, and very lush he was, too!

Cathy called with the best news in the world – she had a good match coming up. The donor in question had the same colouring as me, she was about 5' 4" tall, and weighed about 11 stone (so she was about the same build as me too). The woman was 30 years old, which is older than most donors are allowed to be, but she had already done this once before with a very good outcome (both she and the recipient each had a baby from her first time) so they were happy for her to donate again.

We had an appointment at the OFU to see Cathy. I had to undergo another dildo scan, and to her amazement she could see what she thought were healthy follicles in my ovary.

"What does that mean?" I asked, confused.

"It means you should have sex every 2 days for the next month. You might get lucky," she replied.

This is the classic rollercoaster ride that every IVF couple talks about. Suddenly, after accepting we couldn't have children and working through the emotional and practical processes to get where we were, and after waiting 9 months to be told we had a potential donor at last, here we were being told that actually – if we just kept on 'trying' – we might 'get lucky' after all. Up and up the rollercoaster we went, hoping against hope that perhaps we might be able to have a child naturally after all. Seamus and I both tried to look enthusiastic at the prospect of sex every 2 days. We dutifully performed the necessary act, as prescribed.

At the same time, I was told to stop taking my usual HRT. This wasn't in relation to the prospect of me conceiving naturally; rather, I was given a prescription for two months of other hormones that were to prepare my body for implantation of the donor egg.

At the end of the month, the rollercoaster sped back down to earth as it became apparent that, yet again, I had failed to become pregnant naturally. It was disappointing, but not really surprising. It was also less upsetting this time because we were on our way to receiving the donor eggs in another month, anyway. Natural pregnancy would have been a 'nice to have' but it wasn't something we desperately needed to achieve any more.

If there is any advantage to having an egg donor baby rather than undergoing 'normal' IVF, it's the fact that we don't need to have our eggs harvested. Obviously, I don't have personal experience of that procedure, but my understanding is that egg collection is done under deep sedation, and the woman is left feeling bruised and very uncomfortable for several days afterwards. The procedure involves putting a fine needle through the vaginal wall into your ovary to collect each egg. This means that the more eggs you have harvested, the more times this is repeated and the more bruised the woman will feel.

I understand that the donor who provided 'our' eggs gave a total of 10, so she underwent this 10 times – half for us, and half for herself. She would have also received a whole host of hormones, not only to prepare her body for implantation, but also to encourage the ripening of all those eggs for harvest. In retrospect, although I was allowed no contact with the donor at all – the OFU were careful to ensure that donors and recipients didn't have appointments at the unit even on the same day – I wish I had sent her some flowers through Cathy. The thought didn't cross my mind at the time, and I don't even know if I would have been allowed to do it, but she must have felt like hell after doing this, and a bunch of flowers might have gone a little way to showing that I really appreciated her going through it for me as well as herself.

In comparison, my preparation was fairly easy. Unlike the donor, who had to inject herself with hormones daily, I had no injections – my hormones were either oral or suppositories. Yes, I was a little squeamish about the suppositories at first, but I knew I had the easy end of the deal!

The wonderful woman who gave us her eggs produced some absolute beauties. Of the five eggs we received, four initially produced viable blastocysts (5-day old balls of cells with the potential to develop into embryos). One was apparently grown the quickest and was looking like the strongest, biggest one – we called that one Eager Beaver. Another apparently looked good and healthy, but was comparatively slow – we called this one Slow. The one in the middle was called Normal Norman. Finally, there was one that was apparently very rough around the edges, and we called him Scruffy. So Eager Beaver, Normal Norman, Slow and Scruffy were lined up and ready to go!

Cathy explained that we had the option of putting in one or two eggs. "It's up to you," she said, "but I have to tell you that having twins is a risk – not a perk."

We were very, very tempted to try for twins. The idea of having an instant family all in one go was so seductive! I'm glad we listened, though. Aside from the health risks to the babies, having twins is incredibly hard work. I have a friend who had twins at the same time that I had my first child, and I still think she was Superwoman, the way she coped. She is a tiny woman, barely 5 feet tall, but her twin boys were huge, at about 6 lb each. They were walking by the time they were 10 months old and, lovely though they were, she was forced into being a strict disciplinarian earlier than I was, simply because she had two children to keep safe right from the start. Mothers of twins also miss out a little bit on the precious first few months of having your first baby, when all you want to do is hold him and watch him sleep for hours – you can't do that when you have two of them!

Therefore, we opted to have just one embryo implanted. Eager Beaver was chosen for us, as the strongest contender. Five days after fertilization we went to the OFU to get pregnant. It all seemed a bit surreal at the time. The concept of going to a clinical unit for half an hour and coming out pregnant *is* a bit surreal, don't you think?

Implantation is not painful, but it is a little uncomfortable, and any notions of dignity must be left behind at the front door. As you lie on your back, with your feet high in the air in stirrups, a metal instrument is inserted (similar to the ones used to gain access for cervical smear tests) and used to open your cervix. The embryo is brought into the room already loaded into a long syringe, which is threaded through the instrument and into your uterus.

The sensation made me feel nauseous, and I have since spoken to someone who told me that she did actually vomit after the procedure. It is a very odd feeling to have your uterus invaded in this manner, but it isn't actually painful.

The whole thing was captured on ultrasound scan, so the person doing the implantation could see when the syringe is in the right position. A screen was also turned towards me so I could see everything happening too. The contents of the syringe was released, and this could be seen easily on-screen as a cloudy mist exuding from the end of the fine needle. We actually have a print-out of the scan of the cloudy mist – it's the first picture of our first child!

6.

I might have made this all sound a bit too easy. As if carrying a baby that has none of your own genetic material is a no-brainer with no emotional strings. Of course, that's not true.

I know a woman who had several failed 'normal' IVF attempts. She and her husband eventually gave up, and she was talking to me about it after I had given birth to my first son. The woman in question was still in her early 40s, and I asked her if she had considered using an egg donor.

"Oh no! I could never do that!" she rallied, genuinely horrified at the suggestion.

To some women, the idea of carrying the progeny of someone else's genes is unacceptable. It is obviously a hurdle that has to be overcome if you are to go down that route. Clearly, given a choice, we would all have our own natural children with no technical intervention at all. However, if that is not an option, I am immensely grateful to live in an age and culture that permits me to still bear and have my husband's children, whom I can nurture and raise as my own.

Nevertheless, I didn't want egg donor status to define my pregnancy, or my children. It's not that I was ashamed or embarrassed by what I had done, but I know two other women with egg donor children and, although I wouldn't criticize the way they dealt with their situation, I did always have the impression that it defined them. For both women, for the first year or two of motherhood, whenever they introduced their children to new people they would add, "They're egg donor children," or – more heart-breaking – "They're not really mine". In a way, I admired their candour. I never volunteered the information to anyone outside of my immediate family, and of course to these two women who were in the same situation as me (after their frankness to me, it would have been rude not to!) They were concerned that I was having problems dealing with the donor status of my baby, but that wasn't really the issue for me. I suppose that to some people, it might be a point of interest. However, I don't think that it's really relevant to most people I come into contact with, and it's not something I wish to focus on. I will be eternally grateful to the donor who allowed me to become a mother, but this was going to be *my* baby.

When I was pregnant with my first son, one of my colleagues brought me in a magazine article about the influence a mother's behaviour while pregnant has on her child's health and future. There is actually quite a lot about this on the internet now, but I was enthralled to read that (according to this article) my diet might have had more impact on my unborn child's future cardiac health than his genetic make-up might do; my emotional state while pregnant might dictate my unborn child's mental health. The beneficial impacts of exercise and a good diet, and damaging effects of smoking, while pregnant were of course already well known. However, this article was going further – it was suggesting that my behaviour could actually have more impact that my son's genetic origin. I'm sure you can imagine how exciting this was. I had come to terms by then that the baby inside me did not carry my genes, but here was a theory that I could still have a huge impact on his future health and well-being in a way that exceeded the genes he was carrying.

I am a scientist by training. Genetics has always fascinated me (I have been known to read about it for 'fun'!), and I had generally favoured a nature-over-nurture philosophy. However, this belief was now being challenged, and of course – under the circumstances – this made me very happy!

What I now believe is this...

Genetics is still a young science – DNA was only discovered 60 years ago, and most of what we call 'genetics' has been discovered or learnt in that relatively short period of time. Although we may have unravelled many of the mysteries of the human genome, the jury is still out on many aspects of the influences that genetics actually have on us as individuals. We share 98% of our genetic makeup with chimpanzees; 60% with fruit flies; and 50% with bananas! We obviously share even more of our DNA with other humans, even the ones we're not related to – let's say 99.9%, and probably more in people with similar characteristics such as race and colouring. Therefore, in the question of nature *versus* nurture, what we seem to be asking is how much of an influence 0.1% (or less) of our DNA has on us. Now, don't get me wrong – I realise the human genome involves millions of bytes of information, so even 0.1% of that is a lot of information, but in the greater scheme of things perhaps it suddenly doesn't seem all that important.

I believe a lot of larger people have larger children because they all eat the same fatty foods in the same house. Likewise, I believe a lot of families are sporty because they have always done sporty things together. I believe that if you raise your children with confidence and love, they will grow to be generally rounded beings who are better able to cope with the world when they are older. Conversely, I believe that if you have an abusive relationship with your children, those children will very likely grow up to be abusive themselves.

I hope that the healthy things I ate as a pregnant mother, and the extra gentle exercise I made myself do up to the end of my pregnancy, benefited the health of my son in the longer term. I dream that if my baby mimics my facial natural expressions (my smiles and smirks) the resulting exercise on his facial muscles might actually shape his own face and expressions so he may look a little more like me one day. Most of all, I wish that every minute I spend with him, talking with him, reading with him, singing with him, playing with him, showing him the world, will help to educate and shape him into a young man who can fulfil his potential to live a full and happy life.

7.

Our families had been largely uninformed about my health issues and the problems we were having. They certainly had no idea we were going through IVF of any kind.

Seamus just didn't share that sort of information with his family – he's a man, after all – and they are not the sort of people to ask (thank goodness!) With regard to my own parents and family, I had told only one of my sisters what we were doing and why, and she had been good as gold about keeping my secret for me. I grew up fairly independent of my family (my parents were separated when I was very young so I did not see much of my father until later in life, and my mother lived abroad for much of the time) so I did not have the close, confidante-type relationship that some people might take for granted with their immediate family members. Therefore, when it was all done and dusted, Seamus and I had the task of telling everyone what was happening.

Trying to do the right thing for the baby, who would be raised with the knowledge that he came from a donor egg (as recommended by the OFU counsellor), we realised that key family members need to have that information too. The alternative scenario was to hide the fact until it accidentally slipped out one Christmas, for example. In that imaginary scenario, not only were the family upset about being kept in the dark, but our child felt that his genetic origin was some sort of nasty skeleton in the closet. This was clearly not to be the case. Therefore, the family had to be told – not just that I was pregnant, but how, and why. We wanted to raise our baby to feel safe and confident, and to never suggest that his genetic origin was a negative feature in his life. Instead, I preferred to focus on the kindness and generosity of the woman who had helped us become a family, and what perfect genes she must have given us to produce our lovely baby!

Of course, telling Seamus's family was the easy part. Seamus was the natural, genetic father of the baby growing inside me. His family were ecstatic. Our son was their first grandchild, and they had waited a long, long time for him to arrive. They have been doting, proud, wonderful grandparents to both our boys. Our sons adore them, and love nothing more than going to visit Grandma and Grandpa. They have a strong, close bond, and unlimited patience.

My mother and sisters had varying responses. Part of this was my fault. Although one of them was already in the know, I wanted to let them all know 'officially' at the same time, as soon as possible after the conventional 3-month mark was passed. In an attempt to achieve this, we sent the same letter to them all late on a Friday night, expecting them all to get it on the Monday morning. Unfortunately, the postal service exceeded itself for once and delivered at least some of the letters the next morning, which was the 9th anniversary of my brother's death. I was perceived as callous and uncaring, especially since I stated in the letter that I didn't want there to be a lot of gossip about the baby and the fact he was an egg donor child. Some of my family love a bit of sensationalism, and I was aware that in the right setting my situation could be set up as a nice little secret family scandal – I was determined to prevent that from happening if I could. Therefore, I had included a firm statement in my letter about not wanting there to be a lot of chatter about the baby. Adding to the fact that the letter had been delivered on the wrong day, which caused offense in itself, serious offense was further taken due to this non-gossip stipulation. As a result, if there was any joyful response to the news that I was pregnant, I never heard it! (Since then, we appear to have reconciled our differences. It's an old adage, but a new baby in the family really does smooth over old wounds.)

However, out of all these people, we actually told my father first. I had known for a long time that he was a believer in nature over nurture, so we thought this would be the most difficult one. Funny how wrong you can be, isn't it? We were at lunch together, and Seamus and I started by explaining that the operation I had undergone 3 years previously (which everyone had known about) had caused a premature menopause (nobody had known this until now). We explained how that meant I could not ovulate or have children, and he nodded patiently, obviously having come to his own conclusion on this point, since we had not sired any offspring in our 5½ years of marriage so far. Taking a deep breath, I then explained that modern science was able to provide a solution, and that I could use eggs from another woman to produce a child.

"So that's what we've done, and we've asked you to lunch today to tell you that I'm pregnant..."

He gazed at me, blinked, and tears came to his eyes. He then said the most insightful thing that anyone has ever said to me. "Well, that's great. You can keep your end of the bargain then, can't you."

I think he is the only person who has ever really understood, or at least voiced an understanding of, the pressure I had felt to make Seamus a father. I am still a little taken aback that it was my father of all people who showed this empathy – he isn't really known for his communication skills. I had never even hinted at the fact that I had tried to persuade Seamus to divorce me so he could have children of his own, before this solution had presented itself. My father understood.

8.

I'll be completely honest about the fact that when I said earlier that I was willing to do this, the driving force behind the decision was to save my marriage and keep my husband. As my father put it so succinctly – to keep my end of the bargain. I would not suggest for one minute that this attitude was driven by Seamus. It was all in my head. Despite Seamus's determination to be optimistic about the whole situation from the very start, refusing to ever fully accept that parenthood was beyond our reach, I can look back now and believe that he would never have wanted to leave me, whatever had happened.

"Did you only marry me for a sperm donor?" he asked me once, in frustration.

"No, of course not!"

"Well, that's not why I married you either. But anyway, it doesn't matter because we'll find a way..."

Grrr! It was bad enough coping with my own grief, without having to manage his apparent idiocy and denial. Yet as it turned out, of course, he was right. The option of not going along with the solution, when it finally presented, wasn't really an option at all.

Nevertheless, when Eager Beaver was implanted it was an overwhelmingly emotional experience, and not just because of what it represented for us as a couple. There, inside of me, was a little life that I was going to nurture and cherish for the rest of my life. Immediately, in my mind's eye, I could picture myself with a dark-haired little toddler at my ankles, pulling on my skirt and calling me Mummy.

I don't know if I did it for the right reasons. Possibly not. But having done it, I knew immediately that I'd done the right thing, not just for Seamus but for myself as well.

For the first 10 weeks we remained under the care of the OFU, returning for regular scans (usually with the dildo attachment; amazingly, you get used to it). I hadn't realised that the heartbeat develops so early on and, with modern technology, we could hear the beating heart of our baby when he was still just a tiny little splodge with funny looking bumps for limbs, and what appeared to be a tail. At last, the OFU provided us with an expected due date and discharged us into general practice care.

The expected delivery date made sense to me, but not to everyone else in the world, it seemed. This probably shouldn't matter, and under normal circumstances in a healthy pregnancy (such as I was fortunate enough to have) it probably doesn't. But there must be some situations when knowing if your baby is one week or two weeks overdue/premature would make a big difference. We knew for a fact that our baby was implanted, 5 days after fertilization, on a definite date. If human gestation takes 9 months, surely a due date can be most reliably calculated based on that information. But no, the form-filling clinicians in primary care cannot cope with that. They want to know the date of your last period, then they add 2 weeks, subtract 45.7, multiply it by pi, differentiate the result, mutter their magic words, wave a wand and ta-da! There's your due date.

Okay, that's a bit of an exaggeration.

But only a bit. My due date suddenly came forward by 2 weeks, just like that.

Then I had to go for my 12-week scan. This was actually a little late, because I had only entered primary care management at 10 weeks (which they now thought was 12 weeks anyway), so by the time I had my 12 week scan I was actually 13 weeks pregnant – or 15 weeks, depending on who you want to believe. The thing is, this is a dating scan. The technicians – who are invariably lovely, by the way – measure the foetus growing in your uterus, and based on its length from head to spine they pronounce another due date.

Based on the scan, my due date was changed again, set back by 1 week, meaning I was actually 12 weeks – or 14 – no, hold on... I'm confusing myself now.

In the end, I made such a fuss about this (I don't really know why – it just seemed so ridiculously silly, and perhaps I was easily annoyed, what with the hormones) that my midwife always put two due dates down on my paperwork, whenever anything had to be recorded. Just to shut me up, I think.

The other thing that was a little bit annoying, although there was no outlet for this, was the focus the clinical teams placed on the fact that this was an egg donor child. It was scrawled over every bit of paperwork, and commented on at every stage. I could see the curiosity in their eyes, and for most of them I must have been the first egg donor pregnancy.

"Surely," I said to a consultant doctor one day, "Now I'm pregnant, this is just like any other pregnancy." Even though I was [just] under 40 at the time, had no health problems at all, and was literally blooming with health, I had been retained under consultant supervision for the duration of my pregnancy, rather than being left purely to the ministrations of the local midwifery team.

"This baby is special," she replied.

"All babies are special," I pointed out, possibly a little too petulantly. I had been trying to obtain 'permission' to have my first child at the midwife-led birthing centre, and the consultant was arguing back that I should go to the hospital, just in case anything at all went wrong.

"Yes," she replied, "You're right, all babies are special, but this one is particularly special, don't you think?" Of course, I had to agree. My baby was the most special baby in the world.

I still asked Seamus to drive me to the midwife-led birthing centre when I went into labour, though. Then I had to be transferred to the hospital in a flashing ambulance when we couldn't get the little monkey out of me, so silly, silly Gina… should have listened to the consultant, hey?

9.

I was fortunate enough to have a fairly easy pregnancy with Eager Beaver, despite my age (I had just turned 40 by the time he arrived – bang went my plans for a big 40th birthday party!) I had very little back pain, no indigestion, my blood pressure remained low throughout the gestation, I had no puffy ankles, and in general it was an excellent pregnancy. As far as I know, once the implantation was done, my pregnancy was exactly the same as anyone else's – possibly easier, in fact.

The only thing I suffered from quite badly was morning sickness. Someone has since suggested to me that the IVF hormones that I needed to take to retain the pregnancy in the first trimester might have made it particularly severe – I don't know if that's true or not. However, it did resolve fairly quickly once those drugs were stopped, which coincidentally was toward the end of the first trimester, when morning sickness is supposed to start abating anyway. Seamus was very sympathetic, and he used to bring me two slices of toast in bed every morning, to take the edge off (eating helps to relieve the nausea).

I had read somewhere that it was a good idea to keep a pregnancy diary, and I really wish I had followed that advice. However, at the time, everything was so exciting and intense that I genuinely thought I'd remember every fluttering and kicking detail forever. Yet trying to think back now, it's all just a blur! I remember I first felt Eager Beaver moving around when he was about 16 weeks old. It's an unmistakable sensation, and once you've felt it once there can be no doubt what it is. I also remember that my sex-drive returned with a vengeance around the 4- to 5-month mark. I don't know that that was all about, but I assume the pregnancy hormones all rushing around might have had something to do with it. Alternatively, perhaps subconsciously I was just so relieved not to have to perform the deed for functional reasons any more, I realised that it was actually supposed to be fun again!

I continued working as normal – albeit no longer my own boss, as the company sale had gone through a couple of months before Eager Beaver had been implanted. I made my last overseas trip when I was 6 months' pregnant. The change in ownership status was in some ways a relief, as a huge amount of responsibility had been taken off my shoulders. However, it was in many ways very stressful, due to the rapid and unexpected changes that the new owners were making. I felt a duty to argue against most of these changes at each stage, although I knew I was fighting a losing battle. Having said that, I don't think the stress affected my pregnancy in any way. Overall, I was a happier, more relaxed person – I knew what was important to me in my life, and I was looking forward to getting there!

I had planned to work pretty much up until the end of the first year post-sale, but the new owners moved the company 30 miles from our location and they accepted that I wasn't prepared to do that commute every day in my condition. (Actually, I think they were relieved to get rid of me by then!) As a result, I actually ended up having the last 6 weeks of my pregnancy at home with my feet up. I don't think I had enjoyed so much time to myself since I was a teenager. It was bliss, and I had time to do all the lovely tinkering-about-the-house-nesting things that all mothers-to-be feel the need to do.

The birth wasn't the nicest thing I've ever done, but I won't go into details. I found it hugely annoying – and I still do – the way women seem to love telling everyone else how ghastly their own childbirth experience might have been. Gather a group of new mothers in the same room, and it's like having a group of old army veterans, all comparing and competing for the most gory story they can tell. It's fine if you've already had a baby – you know what it's all about anyway – but if you are yet to have your first childbirth experience, I just think it's wrong and cruel to harp on about the difficult bits. Therefore, may I just say – if you have not yet had a baby – that childbirth obviously isn't the most pleasant experience you will have in your life; the contractions can become painful, and a long labour can be exhausting. However, even in the grips of a 2-minute contraction you must know it won't go on forever and, even though they are painful, the time gaps between contractions are pain-free, giving you a chance to catch your breath. Moreover, after that last push the pain is all gone, and you have a real live baby to hold.

And thus Eager Beaver finally came into the world. We called him Joshua.

10.

I'm afraid that if we are being objective, we have to admit that it is an indisputable fact that almost all babies are not very attractive when they are first born. However, I am yet to meet a mother than can see a single flaw in her own new baby, and I was no exception to that rule. They have been squashed and squeezed and, while some look a bit flaky, Joshua was covered in a layer of fine, silky black hair. It was all over his shoulders and down his back. I used to stroke my little chimpanzee (98% similar genes, after all) and thought it was so cute. Joshua's little wrinkled fingers would wrap around mine, and he was the most beautiful little thing I had ever seen. Seamus and I never wanted to put him down. For the first few weeks of his life, he was held 24 hours a day. We took it in turns to sleep so one of us could hold him throughout the night.

Seamus was incessantly taking photos of Joshua. He told me one day that he wanted a photo of him every day of his first year. I think we might have managed it!

I dedicated myself to motherhood, and I found incredible fulfilment in doing so. Many of my old friends and acquaintances assured me that I'd be bored by the time Joshua was 6 months old; 12

months at the most. They were wrong. I found Joshua endlessly fascinating. He seemed to learn or do something new every day. I didn't want to miss a single minute.

Joshua's first word was "Mummy".

I went every 2 weeks to have him weighed by the health visitor. I never failed to call Seamus immediately to let him know how much weight he had gained in the past fortnight, and Seamus never failed to show a dutiful level of attention to the news.

Joshua first crawled at Christmas, because he wanted to reach the baubles on the Christmas tree. He finally figured out we weren't going to give him one, so he just crawled over and took one himself. We were so proud of him, we let him strip the tree of any baubles he could reach.

Seamus bought him an electric ride-in Alfa Romeo for his first Christmas. It was another 18 months before he could drive it. He still couldn't reach the pedals that summer, but Seamus re-wired the car so Joshua could operate it with buttons on the side, until he was big enough to reach the pedals.

My cousin had lent me a pram, and we never used it even once. Joshua was carried absolutely everywhere, and when he became too big to carry in my arms comfortably (around 6 weeks) he was simply transferred to a BabyBjörn® baby carrier, which held him snugly against my chest. Joshua was cuddled endlessly for the first few months of his life, and he was a gloriously happy baby unless, of course, we ever tried to put him down!

We seemed to have the only baby in the world who screamed every time he went in the car. No-one could understand it – babies love cars, don't they? Hmm... not if that's the only place they don't get a cuddle, they don't! Anyone could see we were spoiling him dreadfully – we could see it ourselves – but we really didn't care. It made him happy to be held, and it made us happy to hold him – where was the harm in that?

He looked so much like Seamus, straightaway. He was obviously going to materialize into my mind's eye's little dark-haired little toddler, a miniature version of Seamus running around my feet. When I was pregnant, I was very worried that Eager Beaver might turn out to be a girl. I didn't believe I would have been able to bond with a daughter very easily. Although I had long since come to terms the egg donor status of my baby, it wasn't something that I thought about every day. Having a daughter – would I have seen her as a miniature version of my egg donor? I am slightly ashamed to admit it took me a while to figure out that it wouldn't have mattered one way or another. Until Joshua arrived I wanted a miniature Seamus. Now Joshua is here, I cherish Joshua for the boy he is. Joshua is his own person, and an absolutely fabulous one at that. If he had been a girl, of course I would have loved my daughter for the girl she would have been. That is what I hadn't understood before I had children. Another case of 'knowing myself better', and the little self-help guru in my head gives me a high-five!

I don't know if all this is typical of a first baby, or whether it was because we had waited so very, very long to have him. Joshua went everywhere in the baby carrier. If it wasn't raining, we would walk to the park and I would chatter away to him all the time while his little head peeped over the top of the baby carrier, looking around him and taking in the world. I cleaned the house with him in it. I hung out my washing with him in it. I even cooked (very carefully!) with him in it. The only thing I drew the line at was ironing. But otherwise, Joshua could have been a living, walking advertisement for his baby carrier.

I think I carried him around in it at least some of the time until he was about 15 months old, by which stage he was getting quite heavy, and he had taken his first steps anyway... and I was pregnant again.

11.

We have a couple of friends in Oxford so in the first year of Joshua's life I think we visited the area a couple of times. Each time, we drove into the city past the OFU and remarked to each other, "Our other children are in there".

When Joshua was 3 months old we received a letter from the OFU letting us know that a year had passed since our 'spare' embryos had been frozen. Sadly, Scruffy had been destroyed, considered not strong enough or sufficiently viable to survive the deep freeze. However, Normal Norman and Slow had been frozen and the OFU wanted to know if they were to remain in the freezer for future use (for a fee, of course). Embryos can be frozen for up to 10 years.

Perhaps a little short-sightedly, I had focussed so much on having Joshua that the idea that I might be able to have more children had not really registered fully with me until this time. However, Seamus and I both agreed immediately that we would like to have another child, a little brother or sister for Joshua.

With the objective of having the second child before I was too old (in my own mind – the OFU had not set any limits to that effect so far) we tried to initiate proceedings when Joshua was about 10 months old. It was all so incredibly straightforward. We called up the Unit and told them we would like to use one of the frozen embryos. The procedure is then simple – we were to go to the OFU for a baseline scan, start taking the drugs again to prepare my uterus for implantation, and then in it pops! A little like the first implantation appointment to get pregnant, the whole thing seemed a little surreal. But reality soon set in for us when our baseline scan showed that I had another large cyst growing in my remaining ovary. With my medical history of a cystadenoma several years previously, this was cause for concern, and it obviously needed to be removed (and tested) before we could continue any further.

Thus, while I should have been preparing a lovely party to celebrate my baby's first birthday, I spent the day before Joshua's first birthday in hospital under general anaesthetic, having an ovarian cyst removed. There are a few photographs of Joshua's birthday, which turned out to be a very small affair – just Seamus's parents, us and a very small cake. Not quite what I had hoped for, but just one of those little disappointments in life that we need to get over. (Yes, I'll get over it one day...!)

I was lucky yet again in that the cyst tested benign, so we were clear to continue with having our second child. However, our plans were set back by a good few months while everything was resolved, and it wasn't until Friday 13th July, exactly 2 years and 1 week after implanting Eager Beaver, that little Normal Norman was finally implanted. As with Eager Beaver, Normal Norman was chosen for us, having been identified by the OFU team as the strongest embryo in storage, and the most likely to survive the defrosting procedure.

My husband was convinced the OFU had a little microwave in the laboratory to defrost the embryos. In his mind's eye, he apparently figured they pulled the little balls of cells out of the freezer, presumably in some kind of ready-meal type packaging, and zapped them for 30 seconds to defrost. In fact, you might or might not be surprised to hear that no microwaves are involved. The frozen embryo is instead moved through a series of liquid solutions, gently bringing it back to the right temperature without damaging its cellular integrity. It's yet another miracle of modern medicine.

I knew what to expect this time, and it was all very functional. The implantation procedure still made me nauseous, but at least I knew this time round that it wasn't going to hurt.

Possibly the only upsetting or annoying thing during the second pregnancy was – again – related to the novelty with which egg donor pregnancies are still treated. Even among the consultants at the hospital, no-one seemed to be able to resist asking whether the new baby came from the same batch of eggs as Joshua. I smiled sweetly as I reassured them that both children came from the same egg donor, and I braced myself to keep smiling as the inevitable comment came.

"Oh that's good. So at least they'll be real brothers."

Don't misunderstand me. In the unlikely event that they need to share a kidney or bone marrow, I think it's great that their chances of compatibility are significantly increased. However, is it really difficult to see why that is such an insensitive thing to say? The insinuation that children from different eggs would not be 'real brothers' can only mean one thing, surely – that I am not their 'real mother'. Isn't this insensitive, or even insulting? Especially from a medical professional? I suppose I should have said something – if I had spoken out and told them how rude they were being (however unintentionally) perhaps I might have saved the next woman in my position from having to undergo the same thoughtless comments and insinuations. I definitely should have said something.

Anyway, despite those little upsets, everything else was fine. I feel incredibly lucky that we hit the jackpot both times. I know a lot of people go through IVF and don't succeed. We had two attempts, and both provided us with perfect little boys. I had another good pregnancy (although any thought of putting my feet up at any point – let alone in the last 6 weeks – when looking after a toddling Joshua was out of the question!) I had the same irritation with the clinical teams changing my due date, and keeping me under consultant care for the duration of my pregnancy. I didn't bother going to the midwife-led birthing centre this time – I just went straight to the hospital, like a good patient.

The labour was quick and easy – Alfie popped out in a fraction of the time that Joshua had taken – and there we had our second beautiful little boy.

12.

Parenthood is largely everything that I hoped it to be, but with a lot less sleep. I think I've been exhausted since Joshua was first born, and I wonder sometimes if I will ever have a full night's sleep again.

Joshua looks just like Seamus and, people being people, they see what they want to see so they all think Alfie looks like me. It's logical and fits into the normal ways of the world, so that's the way people see it. I don't mind. Perhaps those facial mimicry exercises *do* work!

I have made a lot of new friends, and I have lost some old ones. One of the most sensible things I did was join an NCT group when I was pregnant with Joshua, giving me a group of other mothers whose first children were all due within a month of each other. We still see each other regularly. You never forget the other people who text message you encouraging words at 3 am, safe in the knowledge that you'll be doing one of the multiple night-feeds too! Other [childless] friends that I have had for 20 years have fallen by the wayside, unable to comprehend my obsession with two tiny little boys. I am sorry for the losses, but cannot do anything about them right now – we still send Christmas cards, and maybe in another 20 years we'll pick up where we left off.

I never did get bored – at least, I haven't done yet. The idea of being bored by Joshua and Alfie still seems ridiculous to me. How could I be bored by two such active little boys, who learn and do new things every day? However, when Alfie was about 6 months old I did go back to some light work on a freelance writing basis. I actually felt very guilty about it at the time, but in fact I didn't do an awful lot of it, and most of the work I did was done after the boys went to bed, so it didn't impact on much of the time I spent with them.

Joshua is a gentle big brother, and Alfie is an adoring little one. They both like reading books about diggers and tractors, and they love playing outside in the garden. They both like the rain, and they love stomping in muddy puddles. Joshua likes grapes and spaghetti bolognaise; Alfie likes sausages and chocolate. Bath-time is the best time of the day.

Our parents and siblings have all doted on both our boys. To date, they are the only children of their generation in either family, so they are happily spoilt by pretty much everyone. I think my mother in particular has found solace in my boys. Having lost her only son when he was little more than a boy himself (in a car accident), she sees similarities between my sons and my little brother, and it brings to life again for her all the lovely things about having a little boy. My little brother loved digging in the mud when he was little, and he spent hours just digging in the little dirt patch outside her kitchen door – my boys do the same, digging in the raised beds in our back garden, and I watch them from my kitchen window. My mother is happy to play with them in the mud for as long as they wish. Joshua in particular has a strange penchant for collecting snails in the garden, so she traipses around the garden in his wake, carrying the little pot he is filling with snails and letting him chatter away to his heart's content.

My mother was very distant during my pregnancy, and she later told me that she wasn't sure how she had felt about becoming a grandmother, but in fact it was great. Whether this was related in any way to reservations she might have had about my babies not having her genetic heritage, I suppose I will never know. However, since meeting them, she has certainly come into her own, and the fact that my children do not carry her family genes certainly does not seem to be an issue now.

We have recorded our sons' lives on video and camera from the days they were both born. One of my greatest hobbies is compiling video collections and photograph albums of them and their activities. I have a photograph of every single piece of artwork that each of them has ever produced – crayons, coloured pencils, pens, paints, sticky glue collages... I cannot bear to let them go unacknowledged. This has possibly given them an undue sense of the worth of their random scribbles, and I hope they don't go on to appear on some sort of futuristic artists' version of the X-factor with the conviction that they are great artists because their Mummy said they were good at drawing. On the other hand, it gives them a sense of pride in everything they create, and I'm sure that must be a good thing.

We have photos of first smiles, first curls, first roast dinners. My favourite photos are those of the two of them holding hands and smiling at each other. Although all of our photographs are digital, I make a printed photo album at the end of every year with the ones that I think are the best. We always have a lot to choose from, and it is the greatest fun to make.

We have video clips of the boys smiling, laughing, rolling over, sitting up, crawling, walking, learning to ride their scooters and bikes. Their first words, animal sounds, reading attempts and songs are recorded for posterity. Special collections are dedicated to particular holidays, Christenings or other special occasions. We even have video clips of the boys sleeping.

Their lives are captured on camera, and they love looking at the photos and videos of themselves and each other.

When my boys are 18 years old they will have the chance to seek out the woman who donated her eggs to make them possible. I know nothing about her other than her age and colouring, but I cannot help but think she must be an incredible person to have allowed me to have a family. Donating her eggs cannot have been an easy decision, but it is one that made my dreams come true and allowed my husband and me to produce two perfect children. Perhaps, if she wants to, she will look at some of the videos and photographs taken over the years and realise how cherished her gifts have been. I will never be able to thank her enough for what she gave us.

When Joshua was born, I created a book using on-line photo-book software. I tried to write it like a children's book with lots of big pictures and few words. The general gist is that once upon a time there was a lady called Gina and a man called Seamus, who met and fell in love. They had lots of fun, but they didn't have a baby, and they really wanted a baby. So they went to the hospital for help, and the doctors and nurses gave them an egg to help them have a baby. It ends with photos of my younger son, Joshua and so it's called Joshua's Book – I wrote the book before my second son, Alfie, was born (I will soon need to Alfie's Book too, of course). Joshua's Book lives on the book shelf with all the other books, and every now and then we read it as a bedtime story. Therefore, as we were advised several years ago, the fact will always be there, ready to be processed when my boys start to understand the facts of life. Obviously, at some point we will need to explain where the doctors and nurses managed to get hold of the wonderful egg(s), but for the time being I hope we're on the right track.

I like to think that by the time my boys are at school, the concept of egg donor babies will be a little more widely accepted. While I was pregnant with my first son, I met another woman through a prenatal class who was pregnant with egg-donor twins. If she and her family had not moved away from the area last year, our children could have all gone to the local school together. When they had their first sex education class, I like to think the three of them could have stood united in telling the teacher how "That's not how *all* babies are made!" Perhaps there will be other children in his class to do that with – you never know.

13.

So, what of Slow? Surely you haven't forgotten our third little embryo.

At the age of 44, with two toddlers pulling at my skirts and running me ragged, I am afraid we decided that we couldn't manage a third child. This wasn't a decision we made lightly. I already viewed Slow as our third baby, and part of me desperately wanted to have him. However, I was already exhausted, I was only getting older, and I knew that if I had a third child I wouldn't be able to be the kind of mother I wanted to be.

Although I suppose I have focussed on all the positives so far, of course we had experienced some downs. For example, Joshua came down with chicken pox just 2 days after Alfie was born, making our first week at home with our second new baby one of the most difficult of our lives... until a year and a half later, when Joshua came down with scarlet fever, developed complications, and ended up in hospital for 4 days. He lost 25% of his body weight, was invalided for about 2 months, and it took about 4 months to get back to 'normal'. Any children are difficult with any illness (and they pick up an awful lot!) but these episodes were particularly bad. Whenever these things happened I would realise that mothers have two arms so they can cuddle both their children at the same time. Not that ill children like sharing those two arms, but that's another issue! So how do you cuddle three children at the same time? We just don't have enough arms.

Although the grandparents are all very engaged with the boys, Seamus's parents live 3 hours away by car, so we see them once every 6 weeks at best. My own mother lives abroad for much of the year, and when she is in this country she lives 2 hours away by car – we probably see her 5 or 6 times a year, on average. This means that respite from parenthood is rare. Seamus and I go out for dinner without the children 3 times a year – once for his birthday, once for mine, and once again for our wedding anniversary. Apart from that, we have no time away from the children.

Tantrums are really difficult to deal with. The world is united that the best way to deal with them is to walk away, but your own child's cry cuts through you like a knife. Walking away or ignoring their screams and sobs is one of the most difficult things a mother has to deal with. Never surrendering to the tantrum is the only way to reduce the number of tantrums your children will have, but even with the best discipline in the world they will still have them sometimes, especially when they are tired.

It's one thing to never be bored by your children, but that doesn't mean you don't get fed up with them sometimes. They are demanding little things. One of my friends, who also gave up work to become a full-time mother to her little boy, was once comparing the stresses of work-life with the stresses of motherhood.

"The thing is," she said, "Even when you have a really difficult customer on the phone, when you tell them to give you 10 minutes, they understand 10 minutes, but when you tell *them* to give you 10 minutes...!"

There are no lunch or coffee breaks when you are looking after children. There are not even toilet breaks, and you don't get sick leave.

Have I already mentioned the lack of sleep? *Everyone* gets tetchy when they're tired – even devoted mothers.

I don't mean to take anything away from women who have lots of children. I admire their patience, endurance, and their apparent ability to go without enough sleep for many, many years. However, Seamus and I knew that two children was enough for us and – more honestly – we knew that we would struggle greatly with a third.

Therefore, when another year went by and another letter from the OFU came through, asking whether we wanted to keep our embryo frozen for another year, we had to turn that knowledge into a practical decision. This is probably the most awful thing I have ever had to do. My gut still wrenches to think of it. Is it guilt? Is it grief? I can't help imagining the child that Slow might have been, even though I know it's wrong to do so. As one of my friends said to me, "To have a child just because it's there isn't really reason enough".

I knew she was right. If I had viable eggs still, I wouldn't be mourning the passing of every period! And yet...

Anyway, we made the decision, and we both knew it was the right thing for our family.

The question then was what to do with the frozen embryo. Typically, we should have had three choices: 1) offer the embryo to a couple unable to produce eggs or sperm of their own; 2) donate it to medical research; 3) destroy it. Seamus and I both felt that it was karma to offer Slow to another couple. Having benefited from someone else's kindness and altruism, it seemed only right that we should do to the same to someone else, given the chance.

The problem was that we didn't have that chance. After finally making the heart-breaking decision not to have Slow ourselves, but to let another family have him (or her), the OFU called to explain that because the egg was not 'mine', I could not donate it to someone else. The original donor would need to agree to doing this, and they did not think it appropriate to seek her permission to do so. Therefore, our options were only twofold – with neither option giving Slow the chance of a life.

I wish I were a stronger, younger person. If I had been 5 years younger I would have had the luxury of time to wait until Alfie was 4 or 5 years old, and then have Slow. But we knew that by the time Alfie reached that age, and we were ready to even think about a third child, I would be far too old to have one. I'd be nearly 50, for goodness sake.

It seems incredible to me that this is not a situation that might be foreseen. That it is not a box that the donor has to tick. Surely it's simple enough – if the recipient of your many eggs is not able or willing to carry all of those eggs to term, do you consent to your eggs being passed on to a third party? Is that such an inappropriate question to ask? I honestly can't imagine anyone saying "No", if they are already kind enough to donate their eggs to one couple in the first place, but I know I'm looking at it from only one side, and a very emotive one at that. Perhaps it is inappropriate. A bit too much to ask.

In the end, Slow was sent for medical research. I'm not sure I will ever fully forgive myself.

14.

Obviously, I can't say for sure whether the way in which I had children has affected the way I have raised them. I like to think that they are confident, polite and well-behaved boys. I try not to spoil them by giving them everything they ask for, but I have to admit that I often find a way to give them everything they want!

There are pros and cons for having our children so late in our lives. On the positive side, Seamus and I have a level of financial security that our younger friends with children can only dream of. We both had successful careers, in our own ways, and fulfilled many of our personal ambitions before we started a family. We travelled a lot, and saw a lot of the world before we 'settled down'. We are fairly confident about who we are, what we want out of life, and where we see the rest of our lives going. We are feel we have already achieved a lot for ourselves, and we are happy to change gear a little now, to spend the next decade or two devoting our lives to our children. In other words, we are largely satisfied with our lot, and that is a great advantage in allowing us to focus on what we now consider to be important – our boys.

On the other hand, as I have already said, we definitely have less energy now than we did 20 years ago. When my parents had my sister and me, they were in their early 20s. When I think back to my own 20s, I know I had a lot more get up and go back then! There is definitely a reason why we are 'designed' to have our children when we are younger. I have two toddlers now, at an age when I am biologically designed to be a grandmother. It takes its toll, believe me! The vast majority of my 'mummy friends' are about 10 years younger than me – that means I really don't have an awful lot in common with them, other than the children.

I am probably raising my children differently to how I would have done in my 20s too. Although I am firm about manners and sticking to routines, I am lackadaisical about whether they eat their pudding before their main course – provided they eat the whole lot at some point, does the order really matter at this age? If they get themselves dressed, I think that the fact they have dressed themselves is far more important than whether their trousers are on the right way round, or their wellies are on the right feet. There is no such thing as 'too many bubbles' in the bath.

One of my earliest memories is insisting that my mother let me out in the rain at the age of 3, wearing my raincoat and wellies, and carrying my red spotty umbrella to walk up and down our little cul-desac in middle England. I just loved the rain! I remember it so clearly, and as a result – to the horror of my younger friends – I am easy-going about letting my boys go walking in the rain. In fact, I like walking in the rain with them. A bit of water won't melt them!

In other words, I have a different perspective on what I think is important. I suppose I might just be contrary, but in truth I think this relaxation of certain rules simply reflects my age and life experiences. What I hope, and am fairly sure of, is that the fact that my children are egg-donor babies does not affect the way I raise my children.

However, I don't think I am alone in finding that the circumstances under which I had my children affects the way I treat myself. Having gone to such extremes to have a child (or children) there is an undeniable pressure to prove to the world that it was not a mistake. A brave face must always be presented. A happy facade must never crack. It means Seamus must take the brunt of any complaints, because he is the only person I could possibly ever complain to. Anyone else might just look at me and say, "Honey, you've made your bed..."

This is apparently a common problem with IVF mothers. We unreasonably feel that since we deliberately put ourselves in this situation, we have no valid right to complain about the bad days when they happen. In the light of day, I can see this is ridiculous. It's not only IVF mothers who deliberately become pregnant, after all!

There are pros and cons for having our children so late in our lives... hell, there are pros and cons for having children at all. But our boys are worth it. They are absolutely perfect. They always will be.

Epilog

If I have any regret it is that my children will not have my nose. As a typical woman I am just as hyper-critical of my body as the rest of womankind, but I do have a lovely nose. On the other hand, my husband's is a huge lump of a thing. I had hoped that perhaps the donor might have had a little nose too, and passed that on, but whether she does or doesn't, my husband's big-nose genes have clearly won that one!

As for the rest... well, my husband is as messy as they come. If he goes to work in a suit, he comes home in the evening with his shirt-tails hanging out, his hair all over the place, his shoes scuffed, and looking for all the world just like a schoolboy who has been hiding behind the bike sheds all day. But as I walk into the living room one morning I can hear Joshua berating Seamus as he and Alfie clear up their toys.

"Daddy, you have to do tidy-up now", my older son is scolding. "You have to put the trains away when you have finished playing with them."

Alfie is dutifully toddling after his big brother, helping to throw the train track pieces into the toy box, and my husband grudgingly starts to give his sons a hand. He looks up at me as I come into the room.

"Daddy is very messy," declares Joshua.

"Essy", echoes Alfie.

"That's your influence, that is", Seamus grumbles.

Yes. It might seem a small thing to anyone else but, yes, it is! Hurrah!

Also by Gina Hashrard

HELPING YOUR PARTNER TO BE A FATHER
Compared with the thousands of books available for new mothers, there seem to be remarkably few for new fathers. Perhaps this is because – as we all know – men don't like to read the instructions! It is infuriating enough when that gorgeous love of your life thinks he knows how to build that wardrobe without referring to a single page of the 28-page manual ("I've done this sort of thing before", he says, with an air of authority), or when he refuses to stop and ask for directions to the party you were due to arrive at 2 hours beforehand ("I grew up not far from here – I know this area like the back of my hand"). But when faced with the challenge of a new baby, not only have they not read the manual, they don't even have that air of authority any more. This is a collection of personal experiences and advice on how you might help your partner through those difficult first few years. Currently only available through Kindle, it's not a long book (about 6000 words), but even if you manage to implement a few of the suggestions it may help go a little way towards turning your partner into a father, and giving you a little more of the support that you need. Good luck!

Available from Amazon

Gina's *Your Story* series for children

YOUR STORY: HOW SOME SPECIAL BABIES ARE MADE, a book for egg-donor children.

YOUR STORY: HOME FROM HOSPITAL, a book for young children who have been in hospital.

YOUR STORY: GOING TO NURSERY, a book for young children starting nursery school.

Available from Amazon

Made in the USA
Columbia, SC
07 December 2020